Baskets

PIECED YOUR WAY
Hand Appliqué
Machine Appliqué
Template Piecing
Paper Piecing

by
Shirley Liby

To Vicki who suggested the change of
format, and the change to projects for this
new series of books. I hope you like
the new look and the change of content.

The purchaser of this book may make photocopies
of the patterns herein for their own personal use. In
all other cases all rights are reserved. No part of the
publication may be reproduced or transmitted in any
form or by any means, electronic or mechanical,
without permission in writing from the publisher.

Copyright © March 2003 by Shirley Liby
ISBN 1-890952-23-0

For a complete listing of Shirley's books, lectures, and workshops, go to
www.heartshands.com

SHIRLEY LIBY PUBLICATIONS
2808 West Petty Road
Muncie, IN 47304
(765) 282-9561

TABLE OF CONTENTS

Introduction 1

Instructions for paper piecing 2

Project 1   Miniature Quilt with Nine Baskets . . . 4

Project 2   Baskets of Blossoms 6

Project 3   Holiday Hanging 8

Project 4   Baskets of Felt and Button Flowers . . 11

Project 5   Woven Ribbon Basket 15

Project 6   Baskets Full of Cats 17

Project 7   Farmers Market 19

Project 8   Tooth Fairy Pillow 22

Project 9   Gift Basket .24

Project 10 Easter Basket Wall Hanging 28

Project Variations 31

Directions for adding pockets 22

I have always loved baskets. I have made them using pine needles, wood splints, grapevines and many other natural materials. I have made them in the manner of the American Indians by wrapping yarns or raffia around a core of rope or sisal. I have collected them from all around the world and enjoyed the great variety of designs and materials that are incorporated to make wonderful carriers for a wide assortment of uses. In the various books that I have published on paper piecing, I have included a number of designs for patchwork baskets to be made of fabrics and quilted into great projects.

This book contains several projects which can be made with your choice of appliqué, traditional template piecing or paper piecing techniques. No matter which way you choose to work, you can make any design here. All the projects are easy to make and the directions are easy to follow. Dive right in and make yourself a basket, or two, or three!

If your piecing preference is needle turn appliqué, add 1/8" to the appliqué pattern and attach the pieces to the background fabric with your tiny appliqué stitching. If you prefer machine appliqué, cut the fabric pieces to the exact size, spray with a fabric adhesive, and arrange on the background fabric. Stitch into place with the decorative stitch of your choice. You can also use an iron-on-interfacing and cut the pieces to the exact size as the pattern. Arrange the pieces and iron them onto the background fabric. Then you can complete the project with the same treatment as the paper pieced patchwork by adding borders and filling the baskets in various ways.

If you prefer traditional piecing using templates, trace the various pattern pieces from the paper piecing pattern onto template plastic or cardboard. Add a ¼" seam allowance to each pattern. Lay the pattern pieces onto fabric, draw around them with a pencil, and cut them out. Now assemble them in the same order as indicated on the paper piecing pattern.

If you prefer to paper piece, print a copy of the paper piecing pattern for each block you need for the project at your local copy shop. If anyone questions you about copying from copyrighted material, show them the statement in the front of the book giving you the right to copy patterns in this book for your own use. Paper piecing instructions are on the next page for those of you who may be trying this technique for the first time.

Cut out one of the paper piecing patterns that you made at the copy shop. The outer line is the outside edge of your pattern. By cutting away the rest of the paper, you will always be aware of the exact edge of the pattern that you will be covering with fabric. Find the area marked with a 1 and make a fold on the line between area 1 and area 2. Now turn the pattern over. Lay a piece of the background fabric over the pattern area 1, making sure it is large enough to cover the entire area and the seam allowance. Place a piece of the basket fabric face down on the background fabric so the two fabrics cover the folded line and overlap it by about ¼". Stitch on the folded line beginning about ¼" before the line and ending about ¼" beyond the line. All stitches are sewn on the printed side of the pattern but the fabrics are on the blank side.

Open up the seam and finger press. If your seam is too wide, trim it to about ¼". Now fold the pattern on the line by area 3. Turn the pattern to the fabric side, find the fold line, and lay the next piece of fabric face down on this line and stitch it into place. Continue in this manner, making a fold in the pattern to guide you for fabric placement each time. Always be generous with the fabric. The only time I have to rip out a seam is when I try to use too small a piece of fabric! Be sure to trim the seam each time so you don't end up with 4 or 5 layers of fabric when the pattern piece is completed.

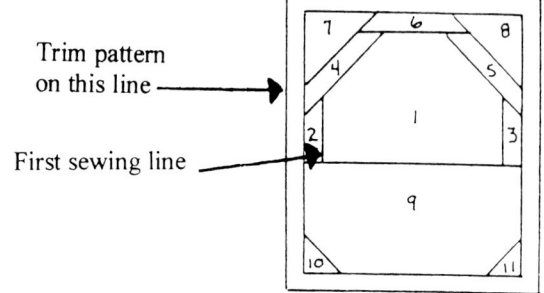

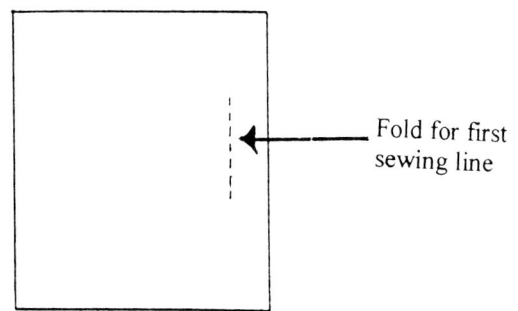

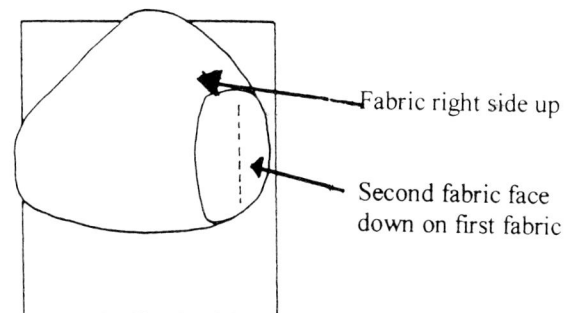

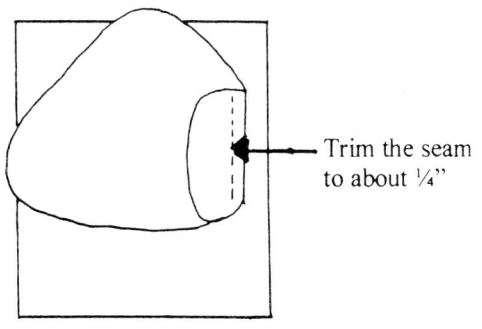

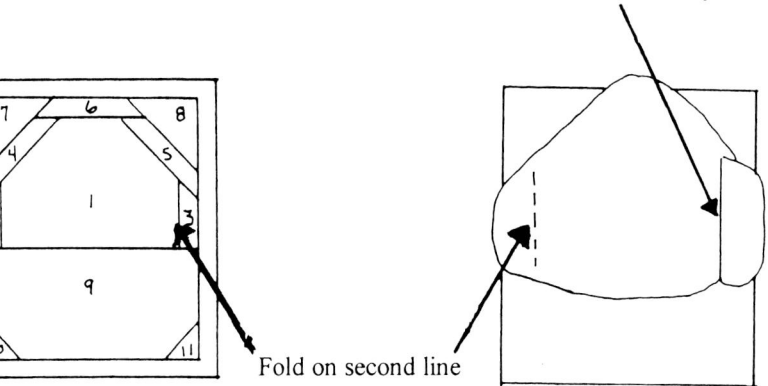

When you have finished sewing on all of the interior lines on the pattern, turn it over and press it carefully. Protect your iron and your pressing board with a piece of paper toweling as the black print may transfer to them when heated. Trim away all fabric that extends beyond the pattern edge. It is not necessary to sew on that inner line, as you will be sewing on it when you assemble the blocks together. I leave the paper on the back for stability until I have assembled the blocks to complete the project.

To remove the paper, lay a large towel over your lap, wipe the back of the assembled quilt top with a damp sponge and place over the towel. Begin at the outer edge and remove the paper one section at a time. Have some tweezers, a straight pin or a seam ripper handy for those little pieces of paper that get stuck in corners. When all the paper is removed it will be on the towel and will be easy to shake into a trash can. Press the completed top and you are ready to quilt!

Remember:
1. Fold the pattern on the stitching line.
2. Turn the pattern over and place fabrics over the fold.
3. Sew on the line.
4. Trim the seam.
5. Open top fabric and press back.
6. Repeat process until all pattern areas are covered.

Please note:
- All seam allowances are included unless otherwise stated.
- The pattern number may be different from the project number.
- All border strip measurements are longer than needed to allow for mitered corners if you choose.
- You should square up with each addition of sashing and borders.
- Paper piecing and template piecing require more fabric than appliqué so be prepared with extra.
- All of these projects are bound with the outer border fabric and the binding is cut on the straight of grain. I usually cut mine 1½" wide. You can use bias if you choose.
- I prefer a light acrylic batting but you should use your favorite weight and type to get the effect you prefer.

Project 1 Miniature Quilt with Nine Baskets
           Finished Size 18" x 19½"

For any of the appliqué techniques use a background fabric 11½" x 13". Appliqué the baskets ¾" from the edge on all sides and space them ½" apart on the background fabric. Once the baskets are applied, follow the directions below to add the borders.

For traditional template piecing make the templates needed by tracing the pieces on the paper piecing pattern. Mark the pieces on the fabric with pencil and cut out. Construct nine blocks and then follow the assembly instructions listed below.

If paper piecing, make nine copies of paper piecing pattern 1 and then construct the blocks on the paper patterns.

Assembly for paper pieced or template pieced blocks:
- Arrange the blocks in three rows of three blocks each.
- Sew the three blocks in each row together with sashing strips between them. These strips are 1" x 4".
- When the three rows are complete, add sashing strips above the top row, between each of the rows, and under the bottom row. These strips are 1" x 10 ½".
- Now add a strip of sashing 1" x 14" to either side of the assembled blocks. Square up the assembled blocks and add borders.

Adding borders:
At this point you are ready to add borders to the little quilt no matter which piecing technique you have chosen. The project shows two inner borders each 1¼" wide and an outer border that is 2¼" wide. I usually sew the top and bottom border strips on first and then the side strips. I press carefully as I add each strip so the corners don't get distorted. Once the borders are finished square up the finished project. It is now time to remove the paper patterns if you paper pieced the project. Layer the top with batting and backing and you are ready to quilt and bind.

You'll need:
- 9 basket blocks (pattern 1)
- 6 pieces 1" x 4" sashing using background fabric
- 4 pieces 1" x 10½" sashing using background fabric
- 2 pieces 1" x 14" sashing using background fabric
- First border - 2 strips 1¼" x 12½" and 2 strips 1¼" x 15"
- Second border - 2 strips 1¼" x 14½" and 2 strips 1¼" x 16½"
- Outer border - 2 strips 2¼" x 18" and 2 strips 2¼" x 20"

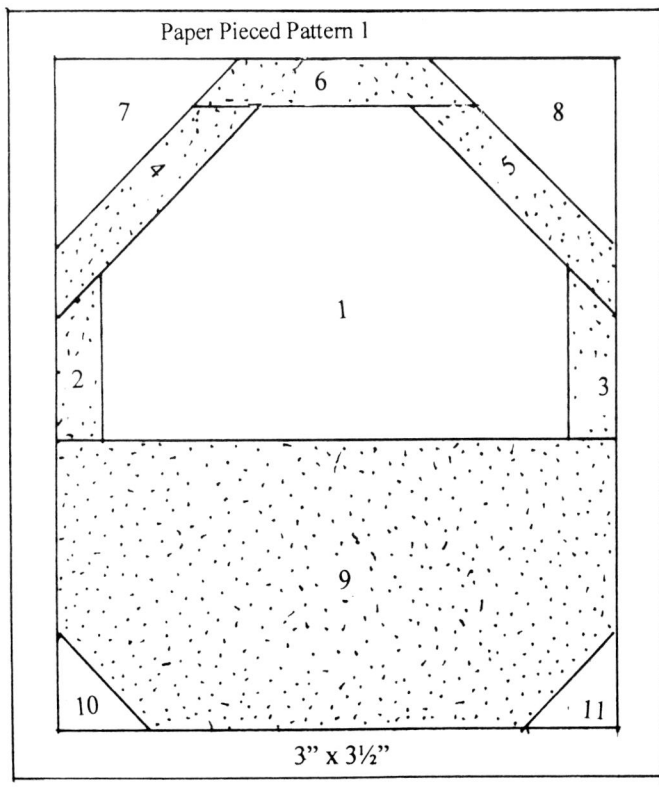

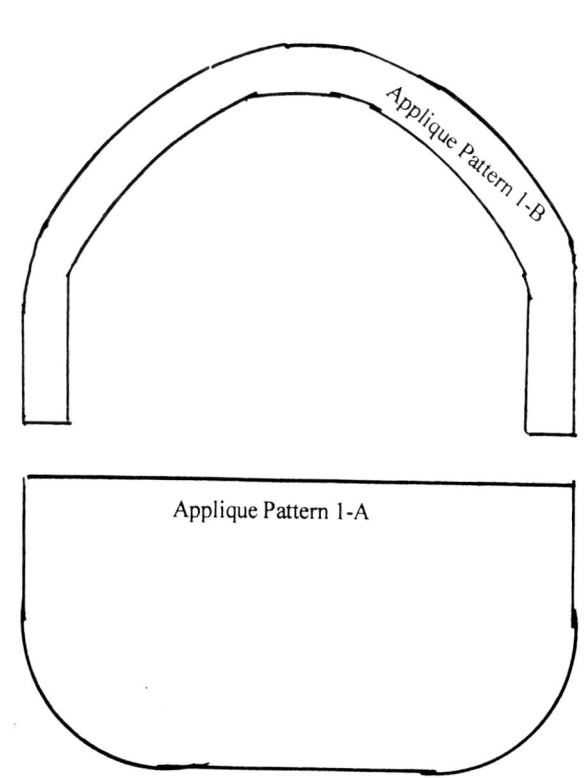

Project 2   Baskets of Blossoms
            Finished Size 15" x 16½"

You will need a 9" x 11¾" background fabric for any of the appliqué techniques on this small project. Appliqué the 12 baskets down from the top edge ¾" in four rows 1" apart. That should put the last row ¾" above the bottom edge of the background fabric. The baskets touch as they are formed into the rows and should set 3/8" inside either edge. Once the baskets have been applied follow the directions below for borders and embellishments.

To piece in the template method, trace the pattern pieces from paper piecing pattern 2 and add seam allowances. Mark and cut the fabrics and assemble them in the same order indicated on the paper piecing pattern. When the 12 blocks are finished, follow the assembly directions below.

If paper piecing, make 12 copies of paper piecing pattern 2 and construct the blocks on the paper patterns.

Assembly for paper pieced and template pieced blocks:
- Lay out the blocks as shown in the diagram on the next page.
- Cut six 2½" squares of background fabric and place them alternately between the inner baskets.
- Cut five 2 7/8" squares of background fabric and cut them in half diagonally. Arrange these in all the spaces around the outer edges.
- Cut one 3¼" square of background fabric and then cut it in quarters diagonally. Place these triangles on the corners.
- The design is now complete and the rows are ready to set together in a diagonal fashion. Begin with the row starting in the lower left corner and sew the blocks together in a row, ending near the top on the right side. Then assemble the rows on either side and continue until all the rows are complete. Then set the rows together. Match the corners carefully to make them fit just right. Try not to stretch the bias edges as you work. Carefully press and square up to be ready for the borders.

Adding borders:
There are two samples of this little quilt on the cover. One is dark with light baskets and the other is light with dark baskets. The inner border on the

light quilt is 1¼" and the outer border is 2¼". The inner border on the dark sample is ¾" and the outer border is 3".

Embellishments:

These tiny baskets are filled with little lace flowers that come by the yard at the local fabric shop. I simply clip them apart and stitch them in place and add tiny beads to the centers. Little folded pieces of ribbon are added to make leaves for a contrast in color. If you can't find a variety of colors in the lace, use a tiny amount of liquid household dye in a paper cup to get different tints on white lace flowers. As soon as the flowers are added, layer the top with batting and backing and enjoy quilting this little project.

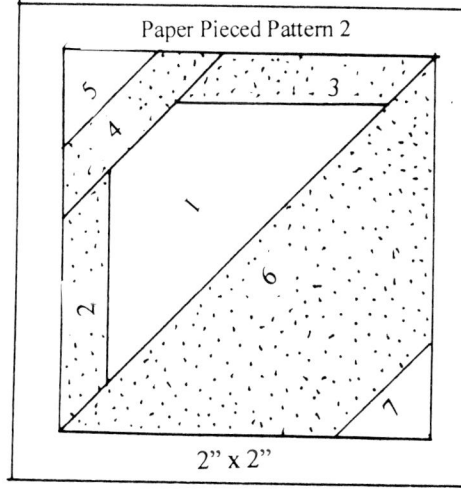

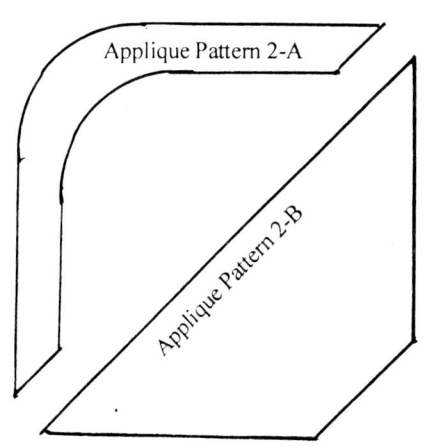

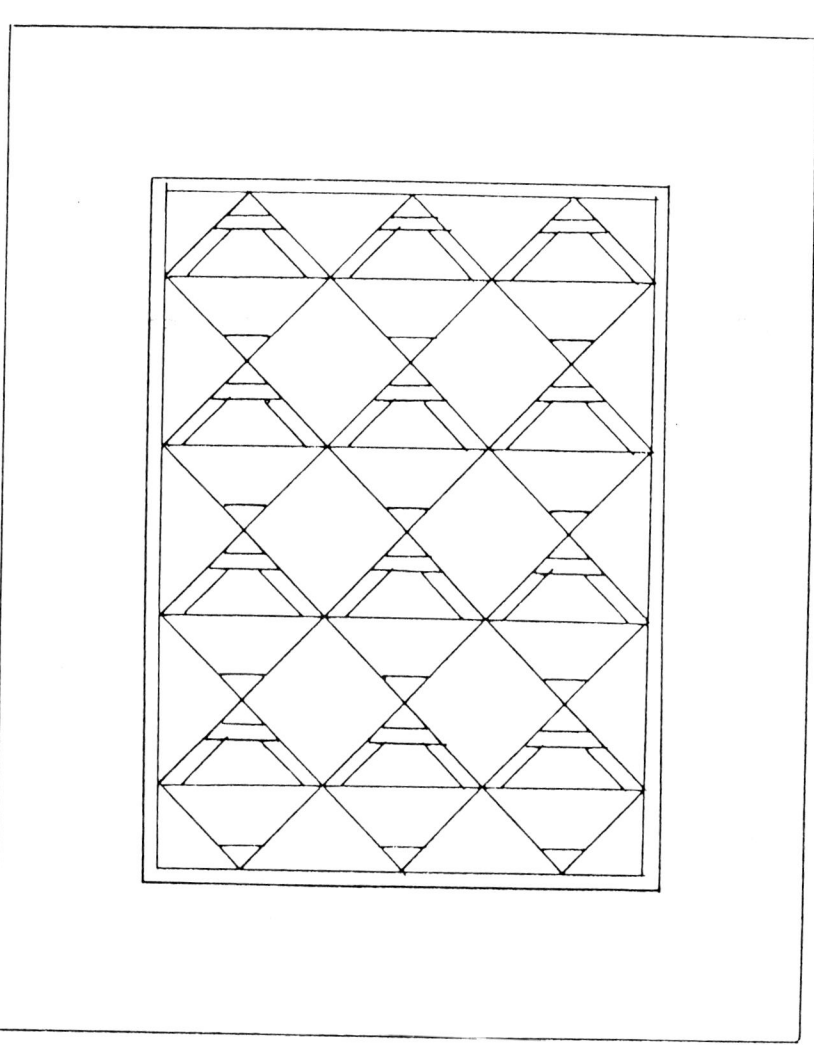

You'll need:
- 12 basket blocks (pattern 2)
- 6 2½" squares of background fabric
- 5 2⅞" squares of background fabric
- 1 3¼" square of background fabric

Light sample:
- Inner border - 2 strips 1¼" x 10½" and 2 strips 1¼" x 13½"
- Outer border - 2 strips 2¼" x 14" and 2 strips 2¼" x 16"

Dark sample:
- Inner border - 2 strips ¾" x 9½" and 2 strips ¾" x 13"
- Outer border - 2 strips 3" x 16" and 2 strips 3" x 19"

Project 3   Holiday Hanging
         Finished Size 10½" x 23"

If you are planning to appliqué this little seasonal hanging, you will need a background fabric that is 6½" by 19½". The three baskets should be 1¼" in from all the edges and 1" apart. Select the little motif you want to feature and "fussy cut" it so that it is centered on the baskets. This can easily be a valentine or Christmas project, depending on the fabrics you select. Once the baskets are appliquéd, follow the directions below for applying the borders.

To piece the baskets with templates, trace the pattern pieces from paper piecing pattern 3 onto cardboard or template plastic, adding ¼" seam allowances on all edges. Cut out the templates, draw around them on your chosen fabrics, cut out the pieces and construct the blocks in the order indicated on the paper pattern. When you have completed three blocks, follow the assembly directions below.

If paper piecing, make three copies of pattern 3 and construct the blocks.

Assembly for template pieced or paper pieced blocks:
* Cut four strips of background fabric 1¼" by 4½" and stitch them above, between, and below each of the three blocks to set them together in a vertical row.
* Add a 1¼" by 18½" strip to each side of the pieced row. Be sure to press carefully as each border strip is added to avoid corner distortion.

Adding borders:
Your little holiday hanging is now ready for borders no matter which technique you used for piecing it. The inner border is 1" wide (½" when finished). Sew it to the top and bottom first, press, and then add it to the sides. The outer border is 2¼" wide. Add it to the top and bottom, press, and then to the sides. If you paper pieced the project, now is the time to remove the paper from the back. You are now ready to layer the project with batting and backing and quilt it.

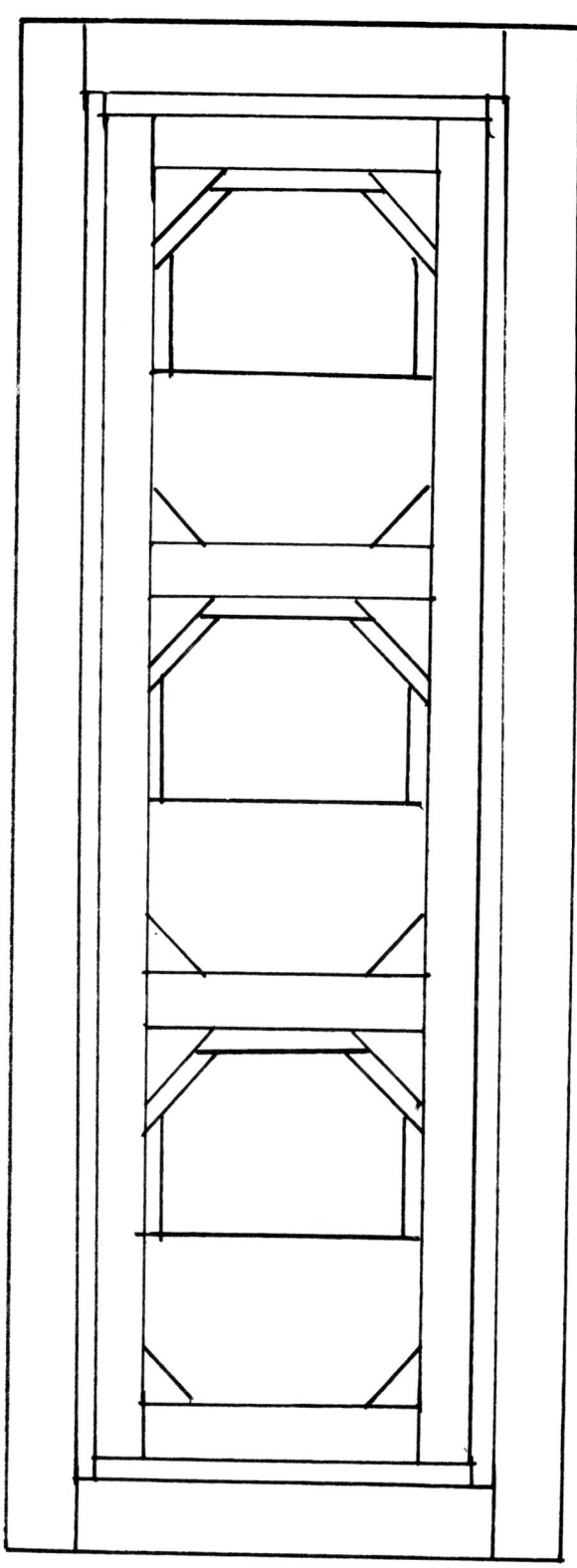

You'll need:
- 3 basket blocks (pattern 3)
- 4 1¼" x 4½" strips of background fabric
- 2 1¼" x 18½" strips of background fabric
- Inner border - 2 strips 1" x 8" and 2 strips 1" x 21"
- Outer border - 2 strips 2¼" x 12" and 2 strips 2¼" x 24"

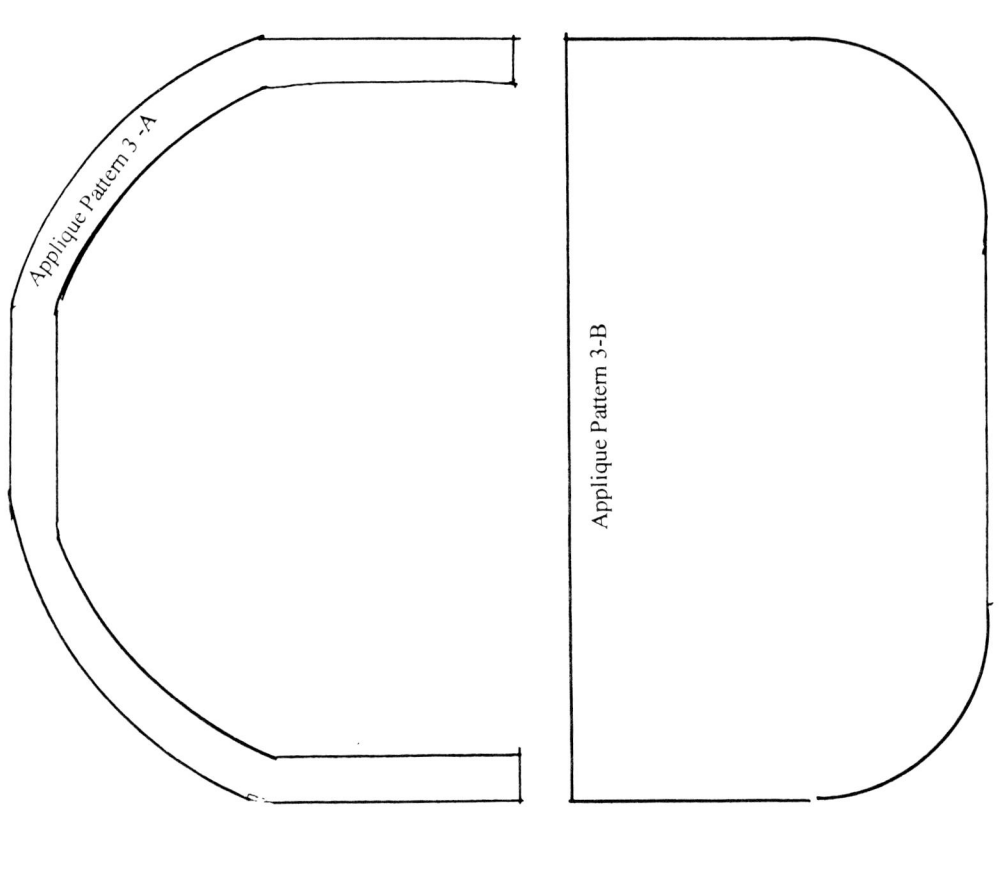

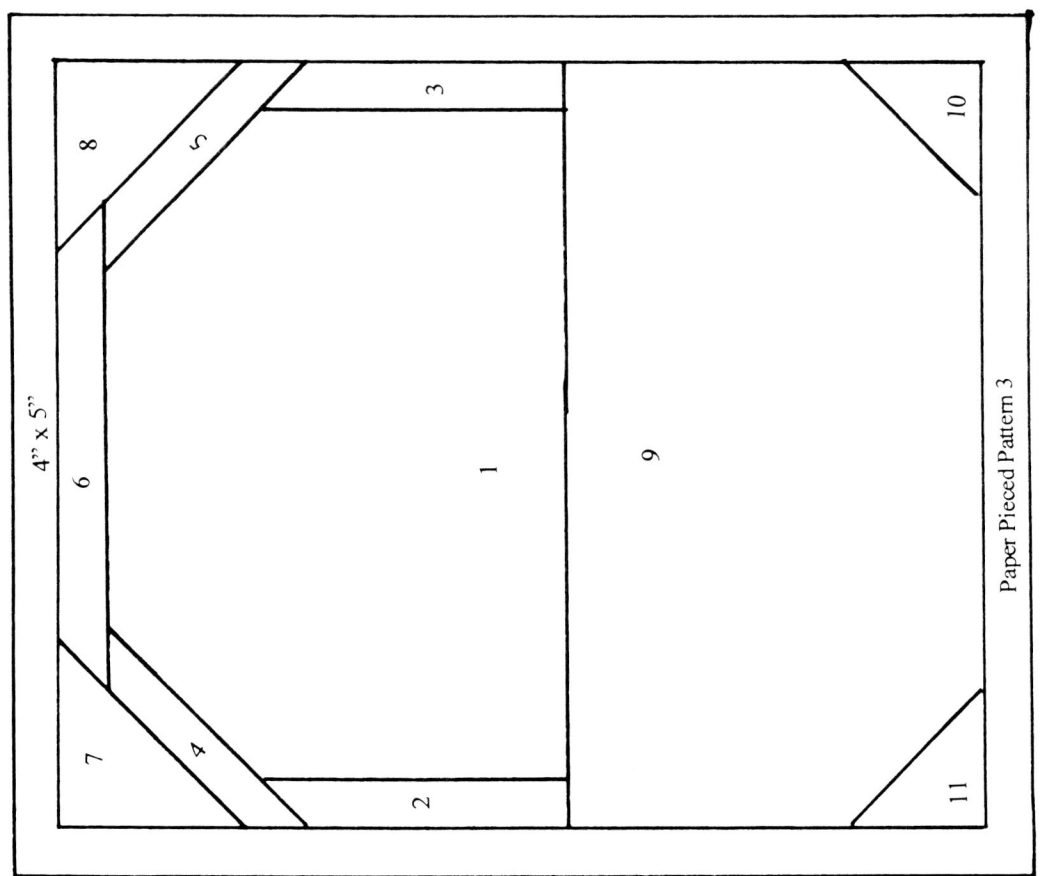

Project 4 Baskets of Felt and Button Flowers
Finished Size 10½" x 24½"

If you are going to appliqué the baskets in this project, you will need a piece of background fabric 7½" by 22". Sew the outside baskets one inch from each end of the background. Fold the background fabric in half lengthwise and crease it so you can set the top basket edge on that fold. The handle extends above it. Fold the background fabric in half vertically and that folded line should be the center of the middle basket. Follow the directions below for the borders, and the felt and button embellishments.

For traditional template piecing, make the templates needed by tracing the pieces from paper piecing pattern 4. Then add ¼" on all the edges. Mark the fabric and cut out the pieces. Construct three blocks and carefully press them. Follow the assembly instructions below to complete the project.

If you are paper piecing this project, print three copies of paper piecing pattern 4 and construct the blocks.

Assembly of template pieced and paper pieced blocks:
* Cut one 8½" square of background fabric and cut it in half diagonally in both directions to form four triangles.
* Cut two 4¼" squares of background fabric and cut them in half diagonally to form four triangles for the corners.
* Lay the blocks and triangles out as shown in the diagram, large triangles between the baskets and small triangle in the corners.
* Assemble as shown and press carefully. Be careful not to stretch the edges as some of them are on the bias. Square up as needed.

Adding borders:
Your project is now ready for borders. Cut one inch strips of a contrasting fabric for the inner border. Stitch it to the top and bottom edges first and press, and then add the strips to the ends and press again. The outer border is cut 1¾" wide and added in the same way. I used the basket fabric for the outer border but you can use whatever you choose. If you paper pieced the project, you should remove the paper now. I added batting and backing and quilted the piece before I sewed the embellishments on.

Embellishments:

The patterns for the leaves and flowers are on the next page. I used five matching flowers in each basket but you can mix the colors and shapes up if you like. I went through my button collection and found a variety of buttons in each color and sewed the flowers on by stitching the buttons in the centers of each blossom. You could use silk flowers or yoyos instead of felt.

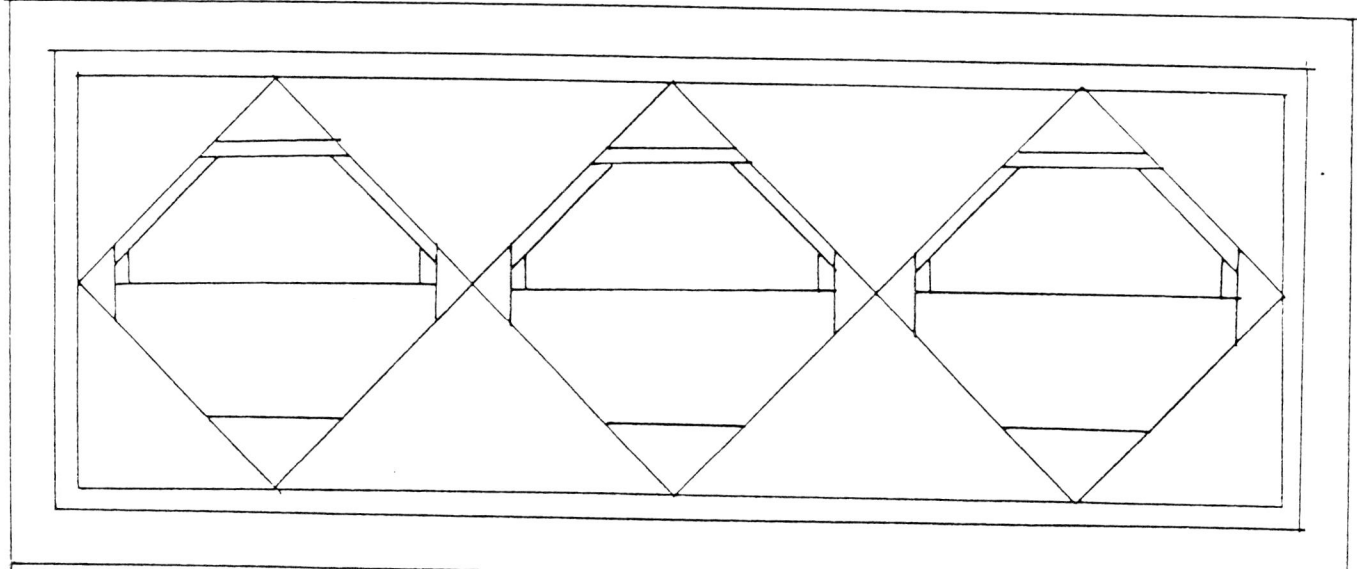

You'll need:
- 3   basket blocks (pattern 4)
- 1   8½" square of background fabric
- 2   4¼" squares of background fabric
- Inner border - 2 strips 1" x 9½" and 2 strips 1" x 24"
- Outer border - 2 strips 1½" x 13" and 2 strips 1½" x 27"

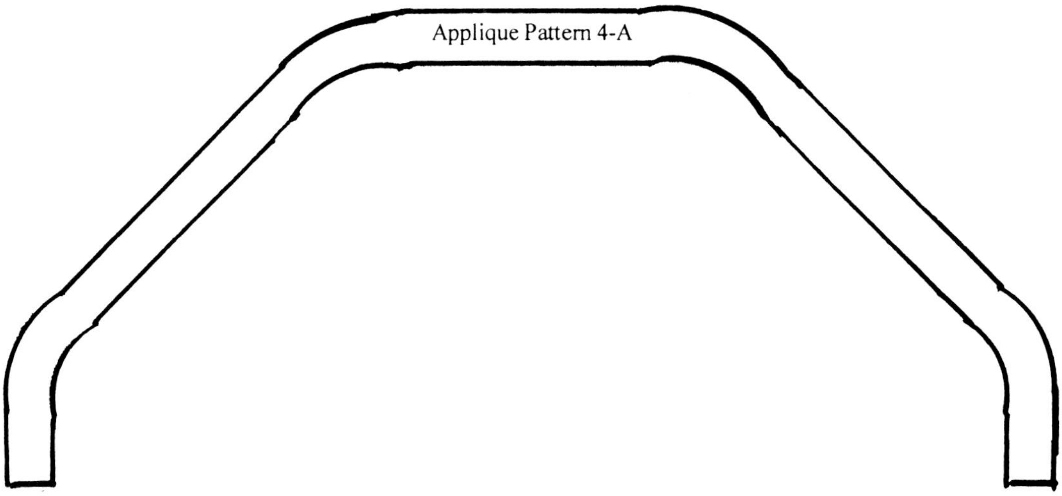

Applique Pattern 4-A

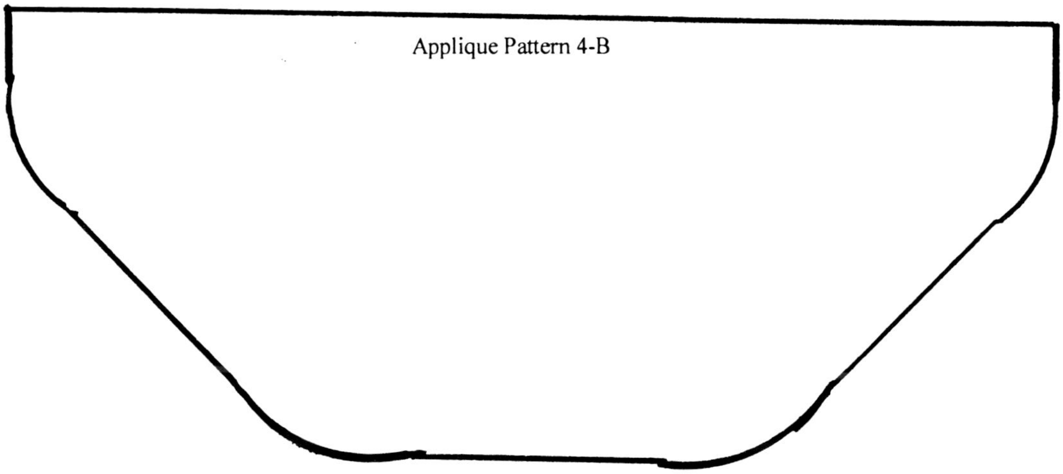

Applique Pattern 4-B

Here are the patterns for felt leaves. Select the shapes you want to use and cut as many as you need for your project.

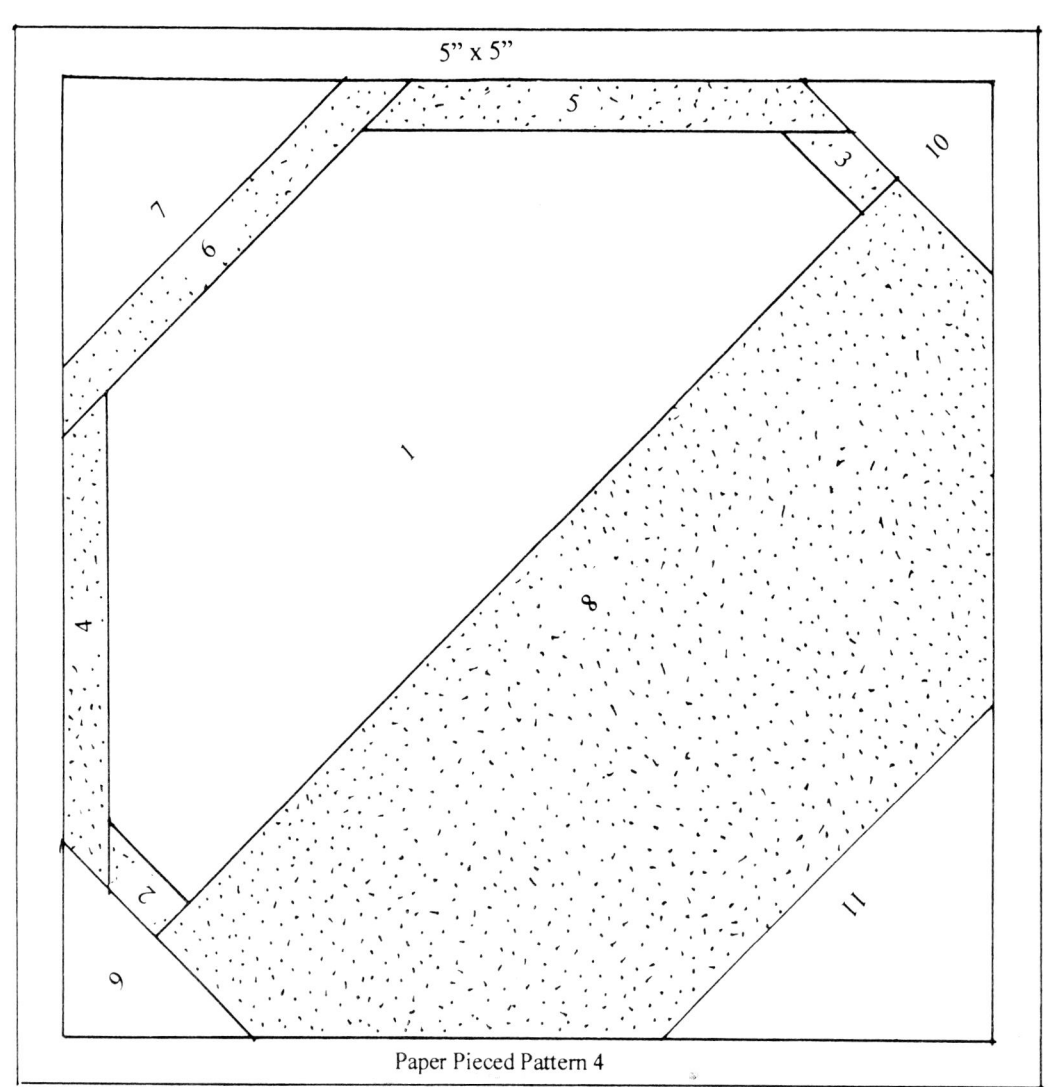

Here are the patterns for the felt flowers. Select the shapes you want to use and cut as many as you need for your project.

Project 5   Woven Ribbon Basket
            Finished Size 14" x 14"

Making the woven ribbon fabric:
Cut a 7" x 4" piece of Steam-A-Seam 2. This product is tacky on both sides and sticks temporarily where you put it. When satisfied with the placement you iron it like other fusible webs. Peel the facing off of one side and pin the webbing to the ironing board, sticky side up. Cut cheap satin ribbon of your choice into 4" pieces and stick them vertically along the 7" edge of the web all in a row like soldiers. Press the top edge with an iron so the ribbon is attached about a half an inch to the webbing. Now cut 7" pieces of ribbon and weave them horizontally over and under the attached ribbons. Weave over where you went under in the next row. Fit all the rows of ribbon up snuggly and weave to the bottom edge of the webbing. When weaving is completed and the ribbons are snuggly aligned, press them according to the directions on the webbing package. Use this "fabric" as you would any other fabric for your basket. Find a matching fabric for the handle. This ribbon fabric will be difficult to appliqué but can be done if carefully basted first. Don't remove the backing on the webbing until you are ready to sew it into your project.

Piecing in an appliqué technique will be easy if you are sewing with a machine satin stitch. Needle turn appliqué will be harder but can be done if carefully basted. You need a 7¾" square of background fabric for the backing. Appliqué the basket in the center of the square. When you have the basket completed see the directions for borders to complete the project.

Make and use templates as indicated in project 4 as this project is sewn with the same paper piecing pattern. Paper piece one block if that is your choice of construction. To finish either block, you need to cut two 5⅞" squares of background fabric. Cut each square diagonally in half to get the triangles needed for the four corners. Press the finished block carefully, square up as needed and add the borders.

Adding borders:
The inner border for this block is made with a 1¼" strip of contrasting fabric. Sew to top and bottom and then to the sides. Press carefully and then add the outer border. This is a 3" strip of the background fabric added to all sides. Remove the paper from the back now if you used the paper piecing method.

You can use this ribbon weaving on most of the projects in this book but make the ribbon very narrow if you use it on the smaller patterns. This block is a good one to repeat in various colors for a larger wall hanging with 9 or 12 blocks and a border. It makes an attractive pillow top too. I trimmed mine with a little bow of ribbon attached with a button.

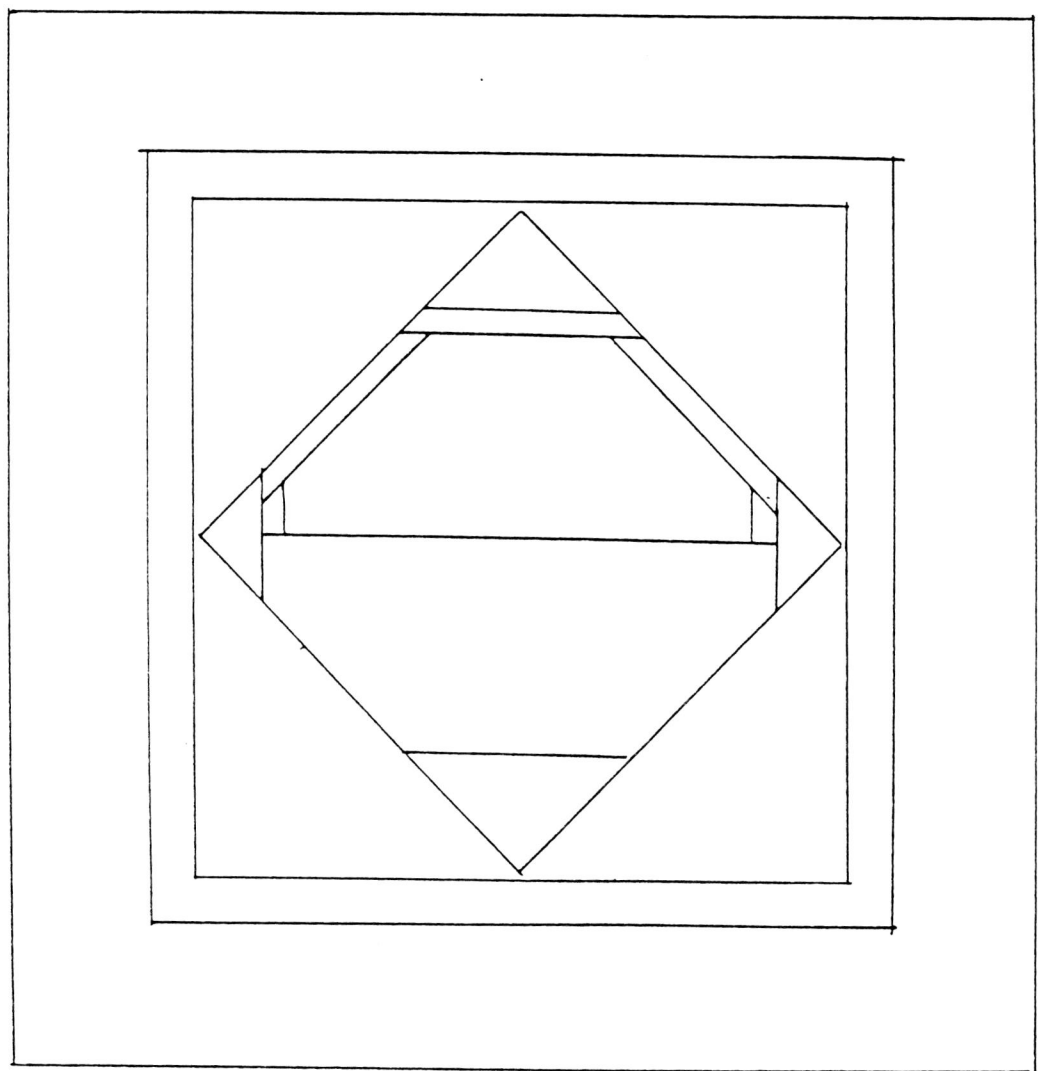

You'll need:
- Steam-A-Seam 2
- 3 to 5 yards of narrow satin ribbon
- 1 basket block (pattern 4)
- 2 5⅞" squares of background fabric
- Inner border - 4 strips 1¼" x 11" of contrasting fabric
- Outer border - 4 strips 2¾" x 17" of background fabric

Project 6   Baskets Full of Cats
            Finished Size 23½" x 23½"

To appliqué this project you need a background fabric 15½" square. Appliqué the four outer baskets in the corners just ¼" from the edge. You might want to cut the background a little larger to make handling it easier and then trim it when ready to assemble the center square with the borders. Center the middle block so that it is aligned with the corner blocks. When this is complete, follow the directions for the borders.

If you are planning to use templates or paper piece this project, follow the directions for making the blocks found in Project 4 as this hanging uses the same pattern. You will need 5 pieced blocks.

Assembly of template pieced and paper pieced blocks:
* Cut out four 5½" squares of the background fabric and arrange them in a checkerboard fashion with the pieced blocks and sew them together.
* Cut strips of a dark contrasting fabric 1¼" wide and sew them to all sides of the assembled blocks. Press carefully and remove the paper pattern at this point.

Adding borders:
Construction of the borders is a little different for this project. Begin by cutting two 10" squares of a light fabric. You could use the background fabric but I found a fabric close to it in color, slightly darker in tint, and thought it was more interesting. Cut the two squares in half diagonally to form four triangles. Add two borders to the two short sides of each triangle. The first border is made from the fabric used for the baskets. Cut eight strips 1" x 11" and sew them on. Now cut eight strips of the fabric that you used around the center section. They should be 1¾" x 13". Press them carefully and lay each of these triangles on your cutting board. Align a ruler along the base of the triangle and trim off the excess fabric. You can attach one of these triangles to each corner of your assembled blocks. Now that the piecing is complete, you can add the cats. I found a fabric with these great cats in a variety of positions and put some in the baskets and some between them. I hand appliquéd mine but you can attach yours with a fusible web and machine appliqué if you prefer. You can put dogs, chickens, rabbits, or teddy bears in your baskets if you like or fill them with flowers like those in Project 4.

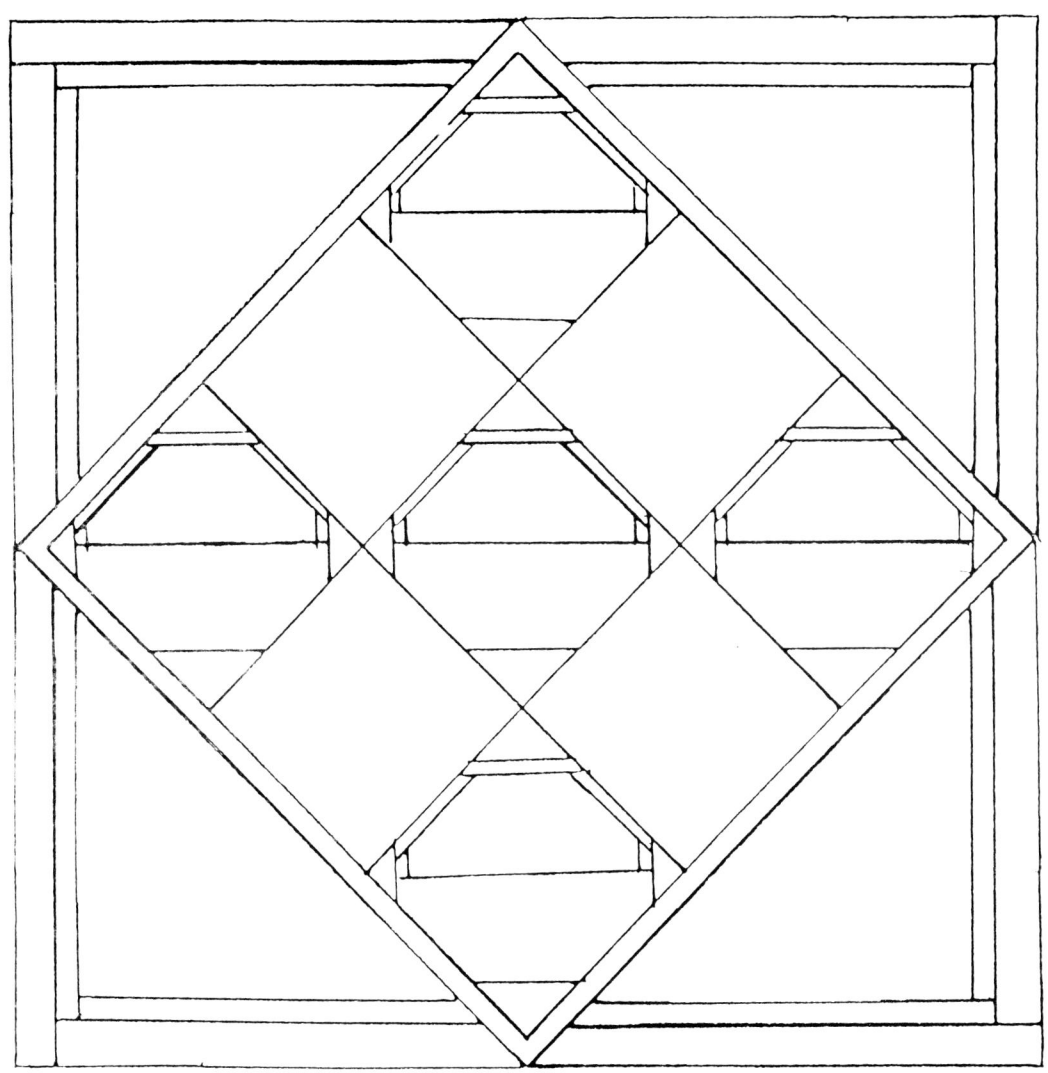

You'll need:
- 5 basket blocks of pattern 4
- 4 5½" squares of background fabric
- 2 10" squares of light colored fabric
- Inner border - 4 strips 1¼" x 18" in dark fabric
- Outer border one - 8 1" x 11" basket fabric
- Outer border two - 8 1¾" x 13" (same dark fabric as inner border)
- Lots of cat cutouts

Project 7   Farmers Market
Finished Size 43" x 19½"

There are two different basket patterns used in this project. One is pattern 3 on page 10 and the other one is pattern 5 on page 21. On pattern 5 there is a dotted line. This pattern is used once in its full size and a second time in the shorter size (up to the dotted line). You will be making four blocks with pattern 3 with handles and a fifth one of the same pattern but without the handle. This gives you a total of seven baskets but only two patterns.

If you are appliquéing this project you have an advantage as you can overlap the baskets and set them in an irregular row for a more realistic arrangement. If you are doing them as shown in the project, you need a fabric piece 34" x 10½" for the background. The row of baskets are set in 1½" from the side edges and 2¾" up from the bottom edge. There are three ½" spacers in the row of baskets. Otherwise the baskets touch each other. Appliqué the baskets and then add the vegetables and fruits. I have been collecting fabrics for this purpose for a long time and have found them in many places. You don't need much of any of these scraps so look for them in odd little places on fabrics in your collection. Once you have filled the baskets you are ready for the borders.

Make the templates needed and piece, or copy the paper patterns to paper piece the blocks. Add the veggies and fruits by using a fusible webbing and iron them in place or appliqué them by hand or machine. "Fussy cut" the pieces so they look piled in a natural way. Once you have the seven blocks completed, sew them together into a row. Cut three strips of background fabric 1" x 5½" and set them between the baskets as shown on the layout diagram. Add a 1½" x 5½" strip of the same fabric to each end of the row. Cut two 3" x 34" strips and add them to the top and bottom of the pieced row.

Two borders are added to complete the project. The inner border is made with strips of a bright contrasting color 1½" wide and is sewn to the ends first and then to the top and bottom. The outer border is a 3¾" wide strip and is added first to either side and then to the top and bottom. Careful pressing at each step will make the borders nice and flat and even. Selecting fabrics is half the fun for this project! If you don't want fruits and vegetables, use animals and call the hanging "The Pet Show". You are now ready to quilt and bind the finished project.
vegetables, use animals and call the hanging "The Pet Show". You are now ready to quilt and bind the finished project.

You'll need:
- 4 basket blocks (pattern 3)
- 1 basket block (pattern 3 without handle)
- 1 basket (pattern 5 at solid line)
- 1 basket (pattern 5 at dotted line)
- 3 strips background fabric 1" x 5½" for sashing
- 2 strips background fabric 1½" x 5 ½" for sashing
- 2 strips background fabric 3" x 35" for sashing

Inner border - 2 strips 1½" x 12" and 2 strips 1½" x 36"
Outer border - 2 strips 4" x 20" and 2 strips 4" x 45"

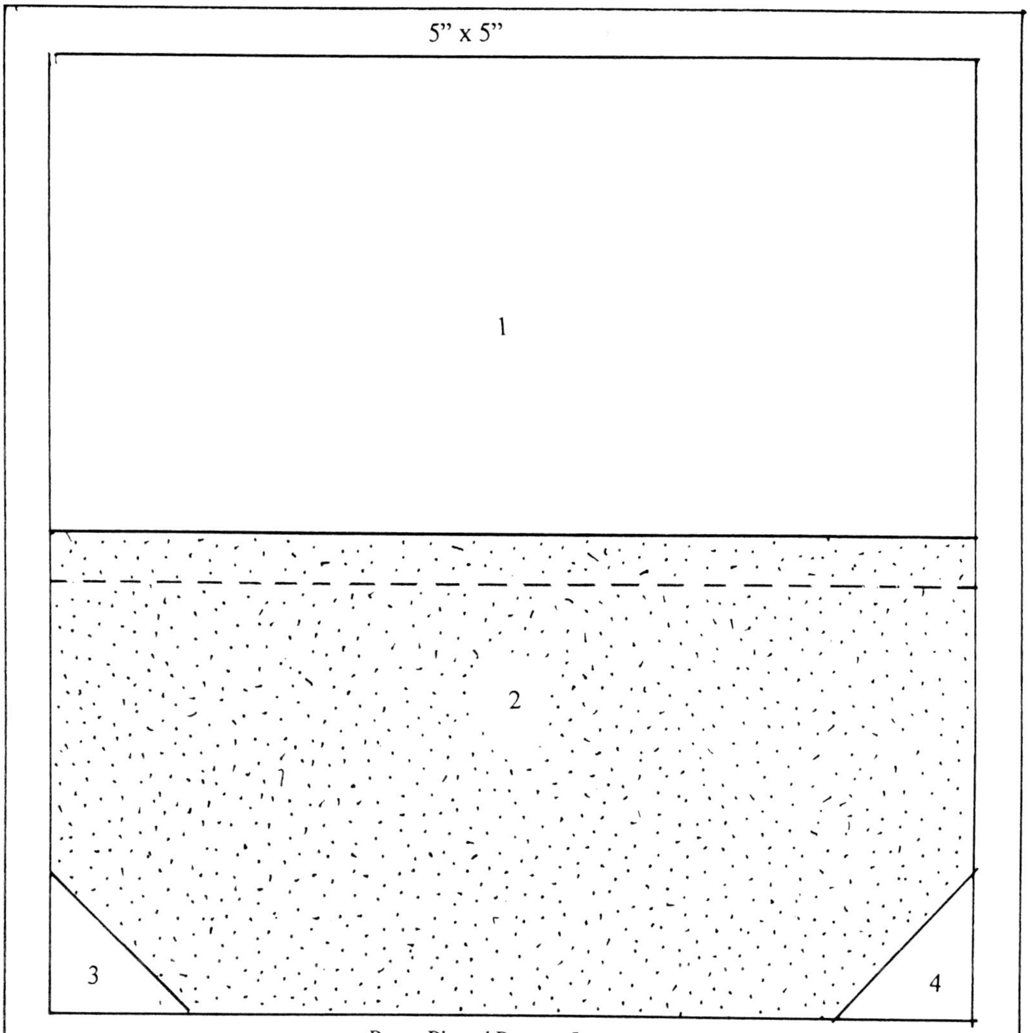

5" x 5"

1

2

3 4

Paper Pieced Pattern 5

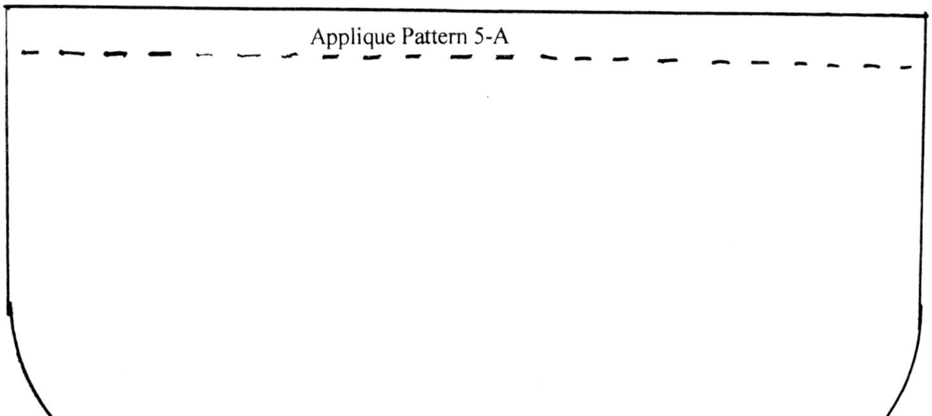

Applique Pattern 5-A

Project 8   Tooth Fairy Pillow
               Finished Size   6" x 7"

I was so lucky to find this wonderful fairy fabric for my pillow. If you aren't so lucky, you can embroider a fairy with cross-stitch. Or you could use your machine and write the words *tooth fairy* in the center of the background fabric inside the handle. Cut out two pieces of background fabric the same size as the paper pattern and set one aside for the pillow back. Appliqué the handle design onto one of them. Make a narrow hem along the top edge of the basket fabric and then cut out the piece and appliqué it to the background leaving the top edge open to form a pocket. Tack the top edge to the handle on each side so the pocket is reinforced so it won't tear off easily when an eager child reaches into it to find his reward.

If you are traditionally piecing this design make your templates from pattern 6 and cut out the fabric pieces. Cut an extra piece of background fabric the same size as the paper piecing pattern for the pillow back. Piece the project up to the point where you are ready to add piece 10. At this point you need a piece of the basket fabric 4½" x 5". Fold it in half and lay the fold on top of the pieced block, lining up the fold with the top edge of the basket. Pin in place and stitch along the sides with a 1/8" seam to hold the folded fabric in place. Now complete the piecing of the block. When finished you have a basket with a pocket.

If you are paper piecing this project, make a copy of pattern 6 and cut a background fabric piece the same size. Piece the block until you are ready for piece 10. Cut a piece of the basket fabric 4½" x 5". Fold it in half and pin it to the pattern so that the folded edge aligns with the edge of the basket. Finish piecing the pattern, adding pieces 10 through 15.

If you want a ribbon handle on the pillow so that you can hang it, add it in this way. Pin the ends of a 10" piece of ribbon to the top edge of the pillow piece one inch in from the left and right sides. The ribbon should lay down onto the basket so that it is out of the way when you stitch the back to the front of the pillow, right sides together. Begin stitching 2" in from the bottom corner and stitch all the way around and back to the bottom. Leave a 2" opening so the pillow can be turned. Remove the paper pattern at this point and turn the pillow to the right side. Press carefully and stuff lightly. Close the opening with slip stitching. You have a great little basket pillow for the tooth fairy reward.

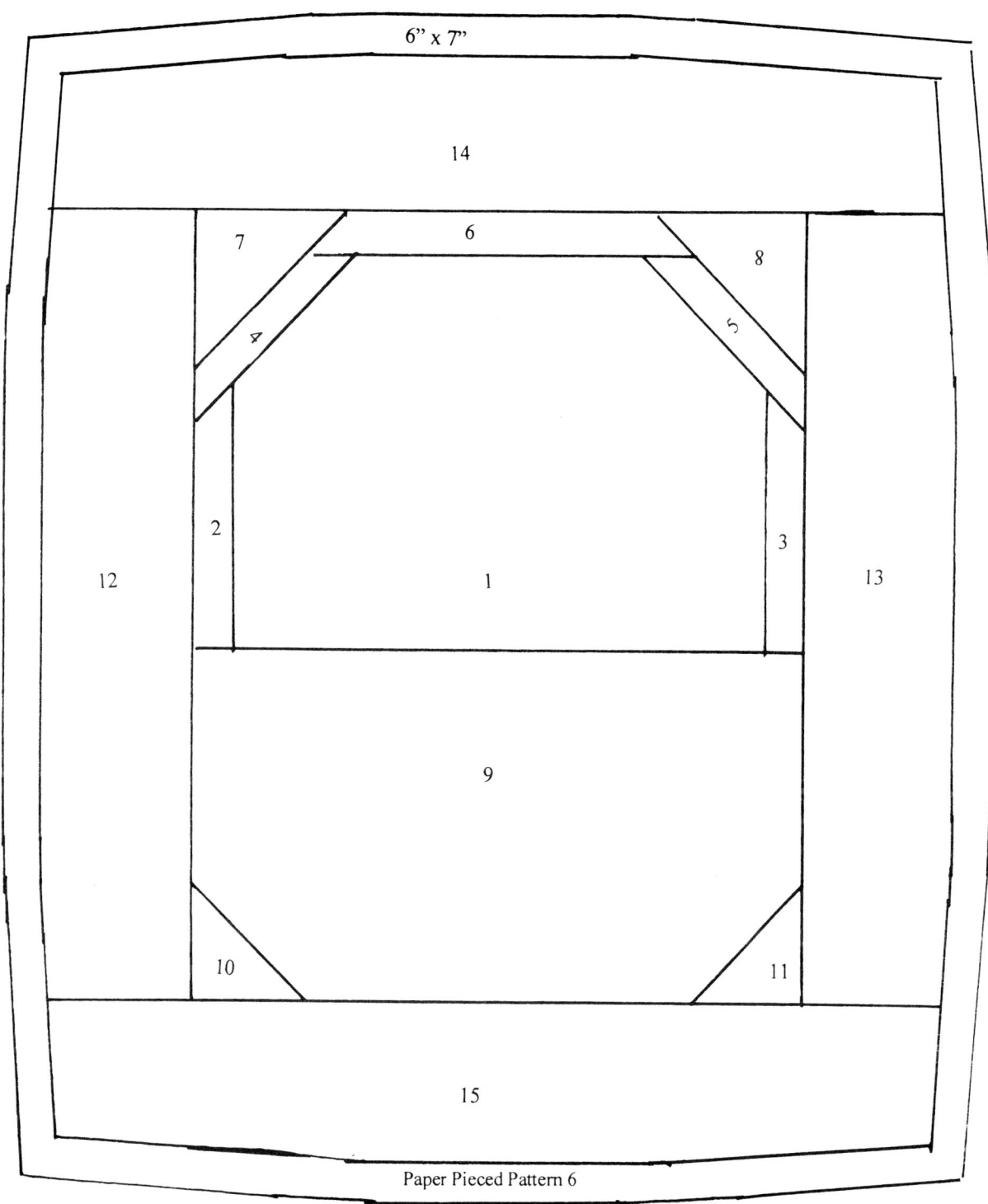

Paper Pieced Pattern 6

You'll need:
- One basket block (pattern 6)
- One piece of backing – identical size
- Fiberfill for stuffing
- Extra basket fabric for the pocket
- Ribbon for handle

Project 9 Gift Basket
Finished size 17" x 17¾"

To make an appliquéd basket begin with a background fabric 9½" x 10¼". Center the basket so that you have a 1¾" edge all the way around it. Applique the handle first. Then make a hem along the edge of the basket fabric and cut out the basket piece. Appliqué it to the fabric leaving the top open. Reinforce the edges where they attach to the handle so they will not break loose when items are put in the pocket. Now it is time to add the borders.

Make templates and cut out the fabric pieces if you plan to piece this project traditionally. Piece the block together up to area 10 and then proceed as directed on Project 8 on page 22 to add the pocket. Once the block is finished add a strip of background fabric 7½" x 2" to each side of the block and a strip of fabric 9½" x 2" to the top and bottom of the block. Press carefully and prepare to add borders.

If paper piecing, make a copy of the pattern and piece it until you get to area 10. Follow the directions for adding the pocket in Project 8 on page 22. Once this is complete, add strips to the edges as described above.

Adding borders:
There are three different borders on this project. Two are of contrasting colors to the background and the outer border is made with the background fabric. The first border is made with strips 1¼", the second border is 1½", and the outer border is 2¼". Press carefully as you add these strips first to the sides and then to the top and bottom of the block. Now the project is ready to quilt.

This great basket has a nice pocket to fill with wonderful little gifts for a friend or loved one. Sachets, lovely handkerchiefs, lace doilies, and little perfumes might be good fillers. Use a theme like gardening and give packages of seeds, gardening labels and gloves. Make a basket full of personal things like a comb, toothbrush, shower cap and personal size toiletries to hang in the guest room or guest bath so a guest has all she needs when staying with you. Select fabrics to fit the theme for this gift or the favorite colors of the person receiving the gift.

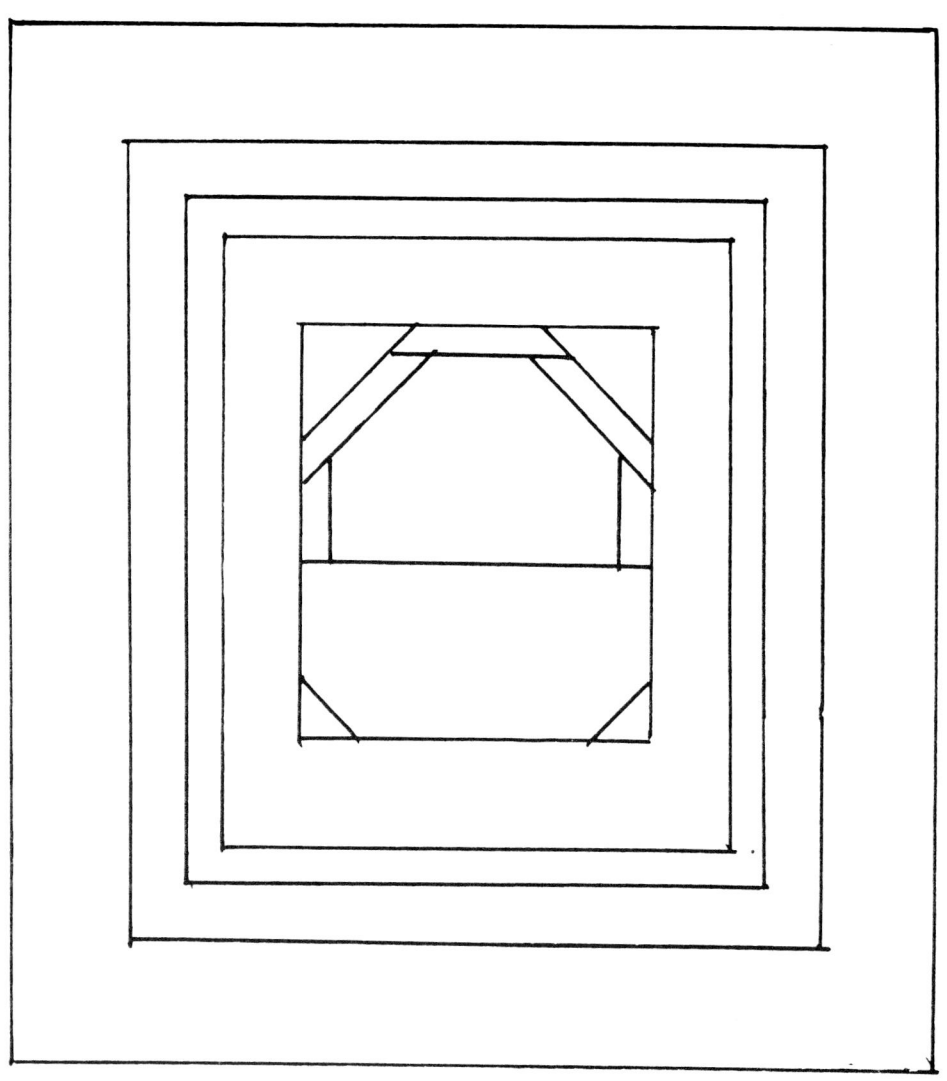

You'll need:
- 1 basket block (pattern 7)
- Extra basket fabric for the pocket
- 2 strips background fabric 7½" x 2" for sashing
- 2 strips background fabric 9½" x 2"
- Inner border - 2 strips 1¼" x 10½" and 2 strips 1¼" x 12"
- Middle border - 2 strips 1½" x 12" and 2 strips 1½" x 14"
- Outer border – 2 strips 2¼" x 17" and 2 strips 2¼" x 18"

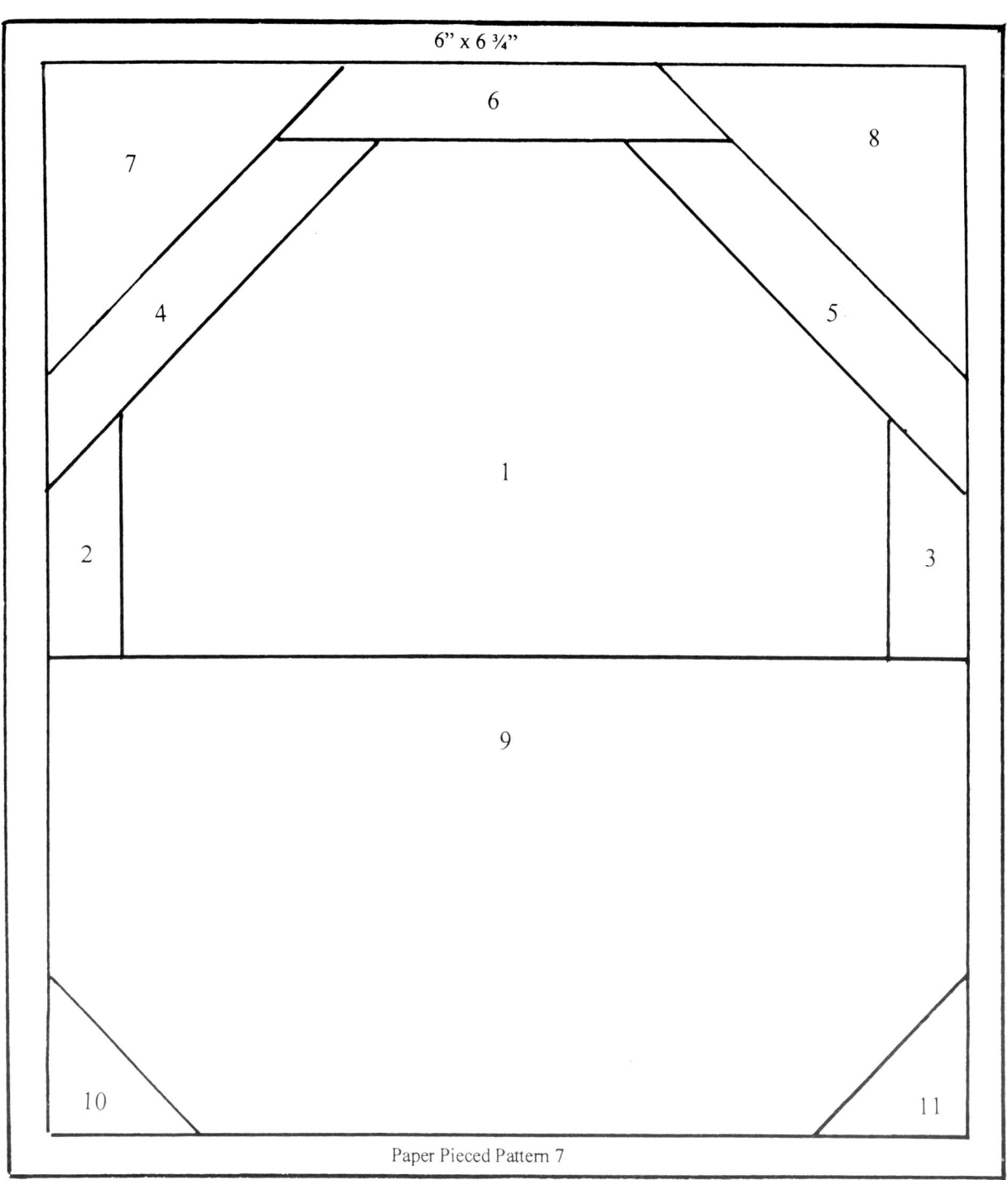

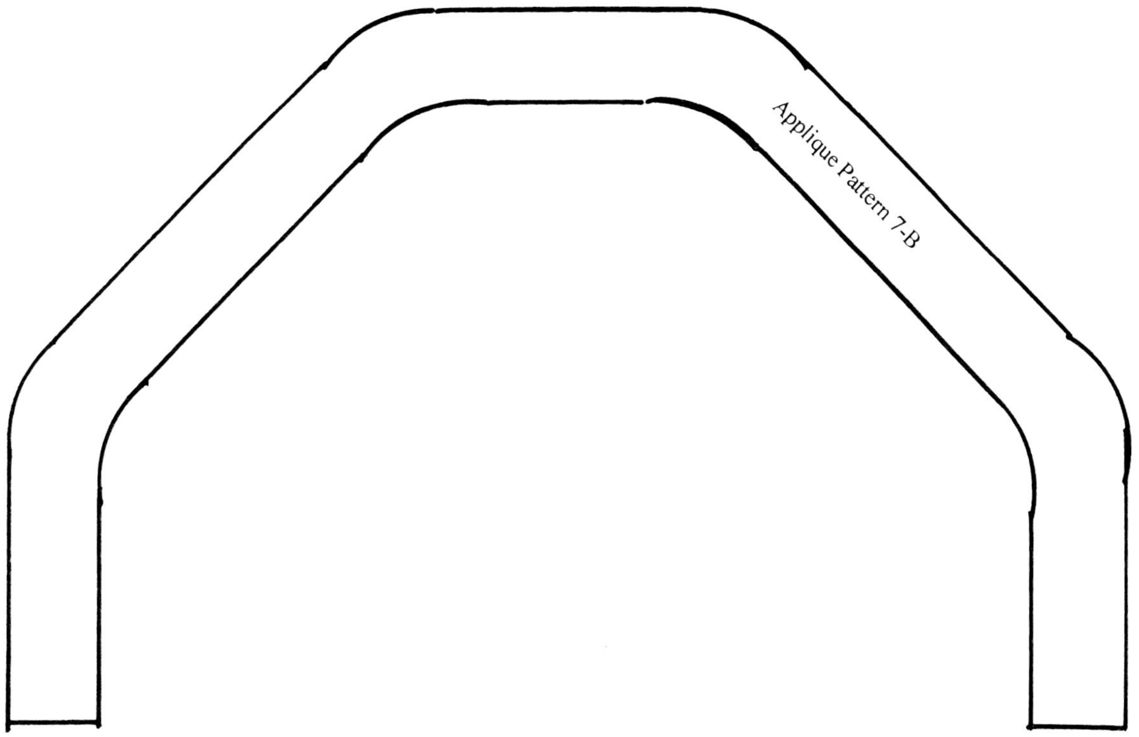
Applique Pattern 7-B

Applique Pattern 7-A

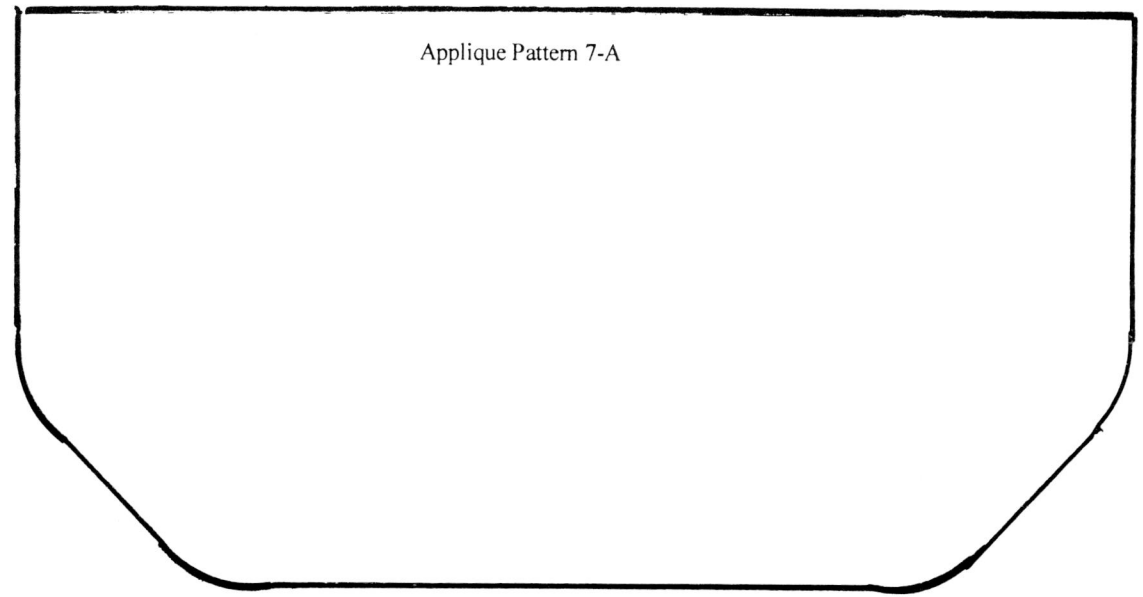

Project 10   Easter Basket Wall Hanging
             Finished size   11½" x 23"

You need a background fabric 7½" x 19½" for any of the appliqué techniques. Set all the baskets in 1¼" from all edges and space them 1" apart. Because these baskets are meant to be pockets to hold Easter grass and Easter eggs, follow the directions for creating pockets as given in project 8 on page 22. You will be using pattern 8-A for these baskets. When you have completed the baskets, proceed to the instructions for the borders.

For traditional template piecing, prepare the templates and cut out the pieces for three blocks. Construct the blocks to the point where you are ready for adding piece 10. Follow the piecing directions for adding the pocket as found in the second paragraph of project 8 on page 22. Complete the blocks as directed and prepare to assemble the blocks into your project.

Paper piecers should piece three blocks up to area 10 and then follow the directions for adding the pocket found in the third paragraph on page 22. Finish the blocks as directed and then prepare to assemble them into the project.

Assembly for paper pieced or template pieced blocks:
- Arrange the blocks in a vertical row.
- Cut 4 strips of background fabric 1¼" x 5½".
- Sew strips of background fabric above, below and in between each of the basket blocks.
- Cut 2 strips of background fabric 1¼" x 19½" and sew them to either side of the strip of assembled blocks.
- Press carefully and remove the paper at this point. Square up if needed.

Adding borders:
Cut strips of a nice contrasting fabric 1" wide and sew them first to the top and bottom and then to the sides of the assembled blocks. Press the border carefully and add the outer border that is made with background fabric. This border is 2¼" wide. It is time to layer with batting and backing, quilt, and bind. Fill the baskets with Easter grass and foil wrapped candy eggs for an Easter treat.

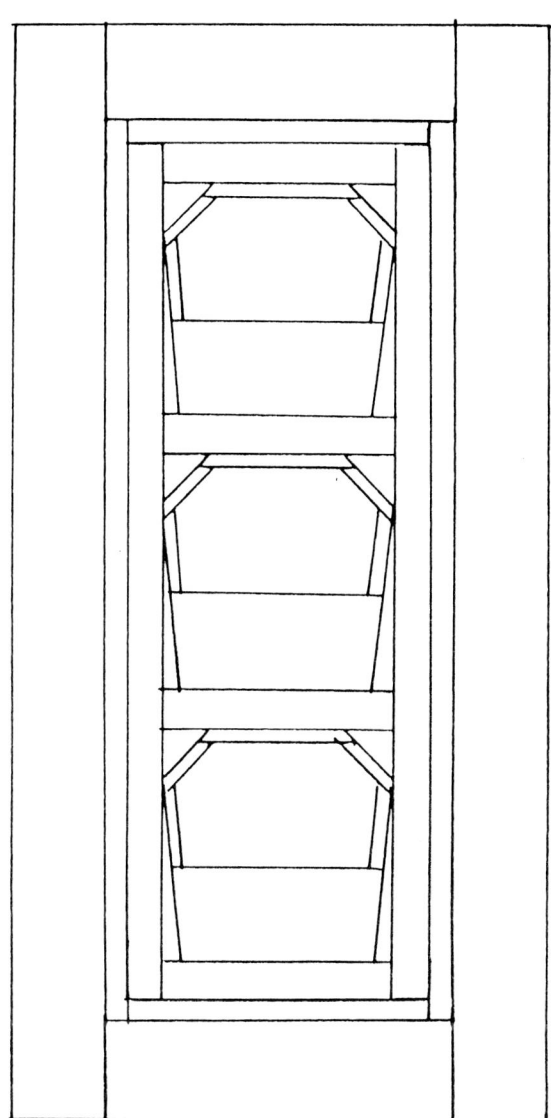

You'll need:
- 3 basket blocks with pockets (pattern 8)
- 4 1¼" x 5½" strips of background fabric
- 3 1¼" x 19½" strips of background fabric
- Inner border - 2 strips 1" x 8" contrasting fabric
  - 2 strips 1" x 20" contrasting fabric
- Outer border - 2 strips 2¼" x 13" background fabric
  - 2 strips 2¼" x 25" background fabric

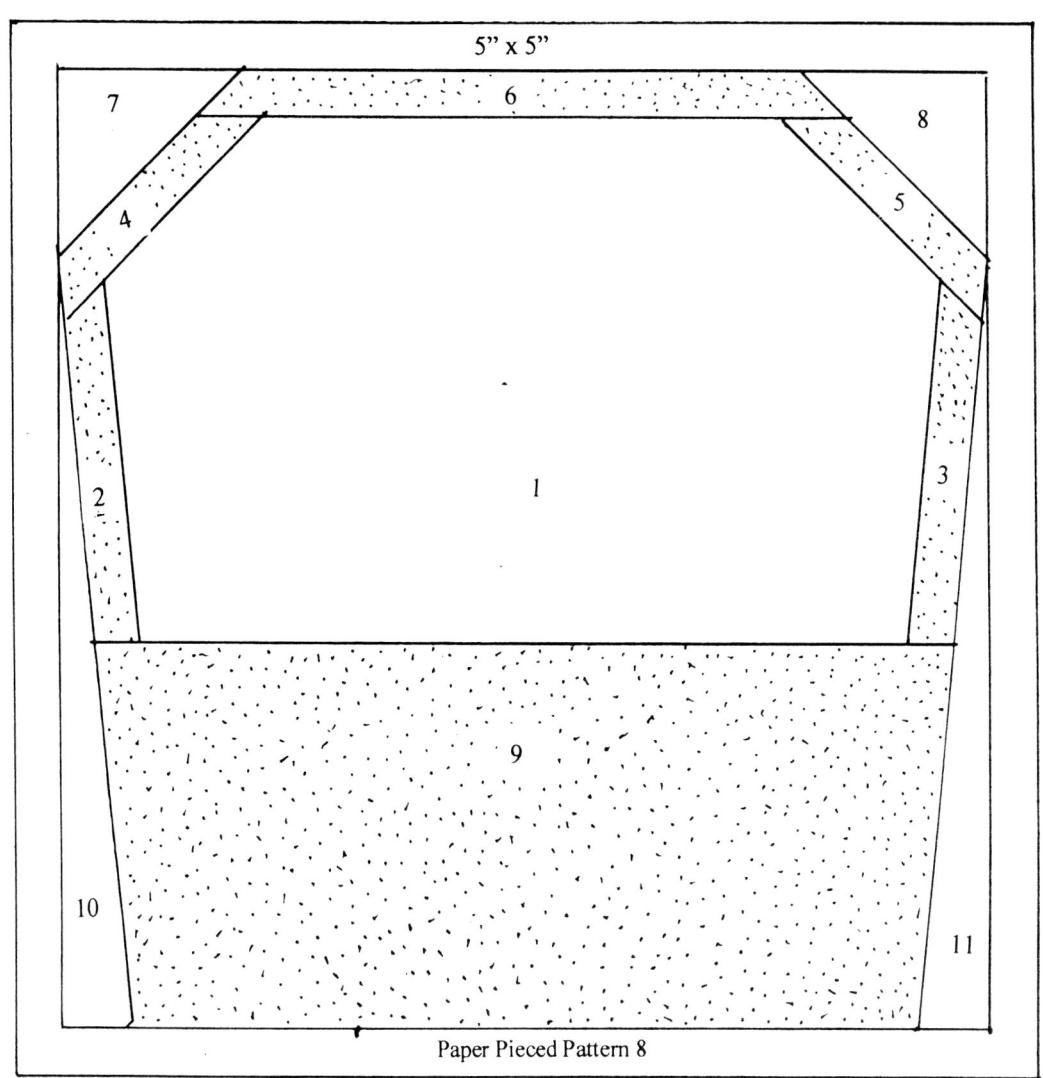

Project Variations:

1. You can add pockets to any of the baskets in this book to give your project a different use. Perhaps you might want to make an advent calendar and fill each basket with a tiny gift in each basket. Simply select a basket pattern and make all the baskets you need to complete your project.

2. Make handles using bias tape or gathered lace instead of piecing the handle in the block design. This is a fun way to vary the appearance of the basket or to "gussie" it up.

3. Fill your baskets with yo-yos or silk flowers instead of felt or lace blossoms. If you use silk flowers, remove all the plastic parts and use only the cut petal shapes. Stitch in the center to attach them to the project. Complete the centers with beads or sequins.

4. Make the baskets into a folk design by cutting the baskets out of felt or felted wool. Stitch either by machine blanket stitch or by hand. Using bold jewel tone colors will help add to the folk look.

5. Make any of these projects into a seasonal piece by changing the fabrics that you use. The Easter baskets become Christmas baskets and can be filled with Christmas cards or candy canes.

6. Reduce the size of the tooth fairy pillow and make Christmas tree ornaments with pockets into which you can place small gifts for family members. This is a fun way to "wrap" your gifts.

7. These can also become little pincushions and you can keep your thimble in the basket pocket. Make the ribbon handle longer and you can wear this handy item around your neck as you sew. This would be a nice gift for a friend who sews or quilts.

I hope you have enjoyed the projects you have made from this book and that the directions have been clear and easy to follow. I hope you like the idea of finding both appliqué patterns and paper piecing designs in the same book. Watch for my next publication in this new series of "Pieced Your Way" books. I have already begun working on the projects and I think you will really like them!

SHIRLEY LIBY PUBLICATIONS

Books on Quilting and Patchwork Techniques:
- Designing With Nine Patch
- Exploring Four Patch
- Borders, Borders, Borders
- Christmas Blocks, Borders, and Banners
- Bible Blocks Old and New
- Miniature Mania
- Color Wash Workbook
- Bargello Basics

Books on Paper Piecing:
- Paper Piecing Patterns
- More Paper Piecing Patterns
- Paper Pieced A, B, C's and 1, 2, 3's
- Paper Pieced Little Landscapes
- Holiday Paper Piecing Patterns
- Even More Paper Piecing Patterns
- Kids Can Paper Piece
- Around The World with Paper Piecing
- Paper Pieced Cats and Dogs
- Paper Pieced Old Favorites
- Paper Pieced Houses and Gardens
- Paper Pieced Sea and Shore
- Paper Pieced Down on the Farm
- More Holiday Paper Piecing
- Border Bonanza

Books in the "Pieced Your Way" Series:
- Baskets Pieced Your Way

All of these books are available from:

HEARTS & HANDS Creative Resource Distributors
826 East 49th Street
Indianapolis, IN 46205
(317) 923-7884   Fax (317) 923-8874
www.heartshands.com